Communion Meditations, Vol. I

Rick Bates

CrossLink Publishing
Rapid City, SD
www.crosslink.org

CrossLink Publishing
www.crosslink.org

ISBN 978-0-9816983-0-4

Cover photo: Spearfish Canyon above Roughlock Falls, Spearfish, South Dakota. Copyright, © 2008 Rick Bates

For Nanci, who for 34 wonderful years

has graciously and lovingly supported

all my foolish ventures and ideas

Table of Contents

Introduction

It is bound to happen. Eventually you will be asked to present a meditation about communion – maybe even during the worship service for the communion time. With this book, you can easily present a unique and interesting meditation that will bring meaning and depth to this most important ceremony.

The best meditations are those you spend time practicing and praying about. Select one and spend several days practicing it, paragraph by paragraph. The best scenario would be to deliver it with enthusiasm and conviction, with minimal reading. Do not worry about word for word accuracy. Remember, your job is to grab the congregation's attention and focus it on the meaning of the sacrifice you are commemorating.

The collection represents some of my favorite meditations. I hope they will bless you as you share them, and we will all see Jesus more clearly as we participate in His remembrance.

Snatching Victory from Defeat

In the 1992 Olympics, Britain's entry, and favorite to win the 400-meter race, was Derek Redmond. But halfway through the semi-final heat, Derek tore his right hamstring and fell to the track. As the other runners raced to the finish, and Derek struggled to his feet to hop the final 200 meters, a man left the stands and rushed to Derek's side. That man, Derek's father, had pushed through the crowd, past security, and jumped to the track.  Hugging his son he said, "I'm here son, we'll finish together." As they came around the final turn, the entire stadium was on its feet, cheering and shouting as Derek crossed the finish line.

The story of Derek Redmond is a great example of triumph over defeat. Something in the human spirit makes coming from behind a championship moment. And right now, this simple observance we are about to share, in a very meaningful and powerful way, recreates and retells the greatest story of triumph over defeat.

As we take the bread and remember the broken body of our Lord, we are together proclaiming that when we fell to the track, the very Son of God stood and rushed to our side.

As we share together the cup which represents the shed blood of Jesus on that cross - the innocent for the guilty - we are showing the world that what we could not do on our own is now within our grasp.

Jesus, with His arm around us, is saying, "I'm here, we'll finish together." We can know with certainty that the stadium of heaven is at its feet cheering and shouting as we race toward the finish.

We All End Up In the Same Box

A sign outside a local law firm read, "Kings and Pawns all end up in the same box." While you might be thinking, "Of course they do!" it is interesting that a law firm of all organizations would post a saying with such an obvious eternal meaning.

Kings and pawns - in this life we are all different:

- Some may end up as doctors; others have no jobs at all.

- Some have much wealth; others have nothing.

- Some have smooth sailing; others struggle at every turn.

- Some are the picture of health; others are disease ridden and undergo long and painful treatments.

- Some have long lifelines; others will see an early grave.

But at the end of our time, according to the saying, "we all end up in the same box."

Individuals without hope, may conclude, "Ashes to ashes, dust to dust." Their interpretation of the saying would be we all end up in the same box ... the 6' under box, and that is the end of the story.

But as Christians we share a dramatically different view of what happens next. Because we know we can never make our way to God, we rejoice that His manifest love made its way to *us*, in the form of His Son.

This morning, as we remember Jesus in the communion ceremony He asked us to observe, we take the bread and see His broken body that was sacrificed for us ... we take the cup and see His blood that was shed for our sins; and, we remember His promise in John 14:2: *"In my Father's house are many mansions. I go to prepare a place for you."*

Yes, we will all end up in the same box – but for Christians it looks a lot like a mansion, prepared with the greatest sacrifice ever, for us to dwell in for all time.

Jesus, the Great Attitude Indicator

There is this great toy, they use in the Air Force, to teach pilots the hazards of believing their senses – it is called the Barony Chair. The students sit in the chair with their eyes closed, thumbs pointing in the direction of motion, as the instructor slowly begins to spin the chair.

It is pretty easy at first ... spinning to the right, both  thumbs point to the right. But, after about 30 seconds of spinning at a constant rate, the body forgets it is spinning and the thumbs point straight up.

Then, the most amusing part to the observers is when the instructor slightly decelerates the chair, and the students' thumbs point vigorously in the opposite direction. Although their bodies are absolutely convinced they are spinning in the opposite direction, the students have dramatic proof to the contrary when they open their eyes and find they have been deceived.

Life is a lot like that Barony Chair. We know the difference between right and wrong and if asked, we could clearly articulate the difference. But once put in motion, with the affect of popular culture and the media, we may be shocked to find ourselves pointing in the wrong direction. It is only by keeping our eyes focused on Jesus and His word that we can keep ourselves stable and upright. Only be accepting His sacrifice, provided to us freely by God, can we be saved.

During preflight in the old days, pilots used to reach down and 'cage the attitude indicator' which meant to align it to the real horizon. The time of communion is our chance to cage our attitudes with Jesus. Jesus asked us to remember Him by taking this bread which represents His body broken for us. The cup represents His blood, shed to cover our sins. As we share in this memorial, let us resolve to keep our eyes on Jesus, not just during communion, but as the one true horizon every day of our lives.

The Image of God

What does it mean to be made in the image of God? How does that make us different from the rest of creation? Those of you with pets could list quite a few ways we are different. For example, you know they do not ponder their family trees, trying to figure out their ancestry. And they could not care less about remembering your birthday!

But, there is something in the human spirit, placed by God, that makes us want to remember and commemorate important events. When Joshua led the nation of Israel across the Jordan River into the Promised Land, they took 12 stones from the middle of the river to the other side. Let us pick up the story in Joshua 4:8:

And Joshua set up at Gilgal the twelve stones they had taken out of the Jordan. He said to the Israelites, "In the future when your descendents ask their fathers, 'What do these stones mean?' tell them, 'Israel crossed the Jordan on dry ground.' For the LORD your

God dried up the Jordan before you until you had crossed over. The LORD your God did to the Jordan just what he had done to the Red Sea when he dried it up before us until we had crossed over. He did this so that all the peoples of the earth might know that the hand of the LORD is powerful and so that you might always fear the LORD your God (Joshua 4:20-24).

But God has asked us to remember the most significant event in history in a very specific way. Before Jesus left this earth, He took a Passover supper ceremony and turned it into a memorial of His death. He broke bread and shared it with His friends, telling them it represented His broken body. And as He shared the cup of wine, He explained to them that it represented His blood, spilled as a sacrifice for all men.

So let us honor our Lord in the manner that He asked, and in so doing, once again proclaim that the hand of the Lord is powerful indeed.

Grace and Mercy

Growing up there were 2 signs of immaturity that we have all seen. They were:

1. The complaint that we did not get something we deserved, and

2. When we have been wronged, the feeling that we did not deserve the treatment we received.

Both are two very interesting feelings of injustice - we rightfully deserved something and did not get it, and we have been wronged but did not deserve it. All too often, it seems like it is all about what we deserve. Have you ever had those feelings?

We can be very thankful that God is a just God, and because He is, God can turn those two feelings of injustice into the most wonderful of blessings for Christians. They are known to us as two of God's most loving attributes: Grace and Mercy.

Here is one way to think of it: grace is getting what we do not deserve – God's riches and forgiveness; mercy is not getting what we do deserve - punishment for sin.

We see both of these gifts powerfully illustrated at the cross:

For as high as the heavens are above the earth,

so great is his love toward those who fear him;

as far as the east is from the west,

so far has he removed our transgressions from us (Psalm 103: 11-12).

As we share the bread and juice of communion this morning, let us give God thanks for the body and blood of Jesus. Because it is only through the lens of His sacrifice that God eagerly gives us His Grace and Mercy.

Unity in Christ

J esus knew His followers would be a lot like you and me ... people from every background, every age group, every nationality, every generation. So before He was arrested, Jesus said a prayer for you and for me. I would like to read that for you this morning, from John 17: 20b – 23:

I pray also for those who will believe in me through their (the disciple's) message, that all of them may be one, Father, just as you are in me and I am in you. May they also be in us so that the world may believe that you have sent me. I have given them the glory that you gave me, that they may be one as we are one: I in them and you in me.

Every year in October, over 1,100 high school students gather for the South Dakota All State Choir and Orchestra concert – an event many say is the largest of its kind in the United States. Here, you will find over 1000 vocalists and 125 of the best orchestra players in the state putting on a performance so moving and so powerful; you would believe they practiced all year together, just for this performance. But the truth is, they met together for the first time the day prior to the concert and pulled it all together. How in the world did they do it?

Well, for one thing, they all had the same score ahead of time … and they practiced from it.

Is that enough to make 1,100 performers sound as if they were one? They would tell you no. The key is in whom they trust to lead them. During the concert you will not see 2nd violinists looking around at the 1st violinists to see what they are doing. You will not see the violas watching the cellos for cues and beats. No – it is all eyes on the conductor. Because, they know that if they can stay in perfect synchronization with the conductor, they will be in perfect synch with each other.

Jesus prayed 3 times in the prayer from John 17 for our unity – just as He and the Father are unified. He tells us He did this so that the world would know God had sent a savior.

We are not that different from the SD high school students who meet together once a year. Yes, we meet once a week, but we too come from different backgrounds and bring different personalities and gifts. But, during this time when we share communion together, it is our chance to put aside the things that make us different, and focus on the conductor. Because it is only by staying in synch with Him – the one who is in perfect harmony with the Father – that we can know the way to the Father.

As we take these emblems this morning, let it be our prayer, that as we get in synch with the conductor, that we would be in perfect synch with each other; and through our unity, our city would know – the world would know that God has sent a savior.

Change in Our World

Benjamin Franklin once said, "In this world, nothing is certain but death and taxes." Many believe that to be true and find change in their lives to be very unsettling.

In fact, large corporations have entire departments dedicated to change management to help employees deal with change. The bestsellers lists frequently include books touting the inevitability of change and how to deal with it. Books like "Who Moved My Cheese," by Dr. Spencer Johnson, use a simple parable to show basic attitudes about change and how to deal with it. There is no question about it; we will have to face change in our lives.

But, in a world that has a lot of angst about change; it should be good news that Benjamin Franklin was wrong about one thing. Hebrews Chapter 13 says it best in verses 8 & 15:

Jesus Christ is the same yesterday and today and forever. ... Through Jesus, therefore, let us continually offer to God a sacrifice of praise – the fruit of lips that confess his name. And do not forget to share with others, for with such sacrifices God is pleased.

So, as we take time to remember our Lord and His sacrifice through these emblems, let us take heart that we are participating in a celebration that Christians before us have celebrated for more than 2000 years; and give thanks that God's provision for our salvation through the sacrifice of His son – a promise as old as creation – is a promise that will never change.

The Good Shepherd

Palm Sunday is when we remember Jesus riding into Jerusalem on a donkey, as crowds of Jews greeted Him as a king. But, Jesus never asked that we recognize Him as a king in that sense. Instead, He described himself much more as a servant ... a shepherd.

A very famous picture of the Good Shepherd, by Warner Sallman, depicts Jesus leading a herd of sheep through a pasture. Three things about that picture are particularly interesting:

1) Immediately behind Jesus, there is a black sheep – one that is blemished and an outcast – one a lot like you and me.

2) Also in the picture, Jesus is holding a baby sheep – a lamb. One not strong enough to care for itself – too foolish to find its own way – one a lot like you and me.

3) Finally, Jesus is shown as a shepherd with a staff – to guide His sheep, to lead them to green pastures, and to rescue them from all forms of evil.

Listen to how Jesus described himself to the Jews:

> *...I tell you the truth, I am the gate for the sheep. All who ever came before me were thieves and robbers, but the sheep did not listen to them. I am the gate; whoever enters through me will be saved. He will come in and go out, and find pasture. The thief comes only to steal and kill and destroy; I have come that they may have life, and have it to the full. I am the good shepherd. The good shepherd lays down his life for the sheep* (John 10:7-11).

Jesus entered Jerusalem as a king - but He led His people like a shepherd. Like a good shepherd, He gave His life that we would be saved.

The Gift of Freedom

It is Freedom Weekend and we look forward to the Fourth of July, fireworks, and parades. We remember great patriots like Thomas Jefferson, Patrick Henry, and perhaps one you are not familiar with -- Lance Peter Sijan.

Lance Sijan graduated from the U.S. Air Force Academy in 1965, and after pilot training was  stationed in Da Nang, Vietnam. In November 1967, while on a night interdiction mission over North Vietnam, his F-4 Phantom exploded and, although Lance ejected, he was badly injured. Lance suffered a compound fracture of his left leg, a skull fracture, his right hand was mangled, and he had a concussion.

For the next 46 days, Lance evaded capture, by crawling at night and hiding during the day. When he was captured he was lapsing in and out of consciousness, but that did not stop him from overpowering his guard a few days later and crawling off into the jungle. He was captured a half-day later and eventually taken to the Hanoi Hilton.

When Lance was united with other American prisoners, he had been so tortured and was so emaciated, that a squadron mate of his from the Academy could not even recognize him. He never complained about his injuries or torture sessions; instead, he continually asked about camp security and how they could plan an escape from their captors.

Before long, Lance developed pneumonia and died in January of 1968. No one knew his remarkable story until the POWs returned in 1973 and told how inspired they were by Lance's courage and intense passion for freedom. In 1976, Lance Sijan of Milwaukee, Wisconsin was awarded the Congressional Medal of Honor.

The human spirit can be fiercely determined and accomplish the nearly impossible. We take pride in that determination and celebrate the stories of people like Lance Sijan. But despite all of that, there is one thing that it is absolutely impossible for us to do … and that is to find our way to God. No matter how hard we try or how determined we are, there is no way for us to overcome the slavery of sin on our own.

But God provided the way in the form of His Son; although Jesus was tortured on the cross, God did not interfere with His mission to provide a sacrifice for our sin and a freedom that leads us back to God.

It is His body that we remember today with this bread, and His blood that we celebrate with this juice. As we share this memorial together this morning, let us give thanks for that sacrifice. For that is the true and enduring gift of freedom.

It's a Small World After All

When you discover you have something in common with an acquaintance or newly found friend, sure as the world, one of you will declare what a small world we live in!

It must have seemed really small to a slave from Colosse, who stole from his master and fled 1,200 miles away to Rome where no one knew him. He met a Christian man who led him to become a follower of Jesus. The slave's name was Onesimus (O-nay-se-mus), and the Christian who befriended him was the apostle Paul. It turns out the slave's former master was a friend of Paul's named Philemon. Imagine how shocked Onesimus was when he put all those pieces together!

In the book of Philemon, we read from the text that Paul wrote to Philemon on behalf of Onesimus in verses 18 & 19: *"If he has done you any wrong or owes you anything, charge it to me. I, Paul, am writing this with my own hand. I will pay it back – not to mention that you owe me your very self."* Here we have Paul not only pleading for Onesimus, but offering to take all of his debt and punishment on himself.

We are a lot like Onesimus: bankrupt with nothing of our own, running from the truth. And just as the Apostle Paul was a mediator for Onesimus, Jesus Christ is our mediator, taking the punishment for our wrongs, and making payment for our sins that we could never make.

He stood before God and declared that if there is any debt to be paid for our sins – put it on His account. Jesus went to the cross, taking our debt and punishment on himself.

As we share these emblems representing payment for our sin, let us be thankful for God's gift of His son – a gift given to cover our wrongs, a gift given to restore us to God.

Oxygen for the Soul

Pilots in the US Air Force undergo yearly altitude chamber rides. The altitude chamber is really just a room with benches, and pilots dress up in flight gear and helmets for the training. Once inside, the air is removed from the room to simulate flying aloft in an unpressurized aircraft.

At various altitudes, the pilots are asked to removed their oxygen masks and perform simple tasks, including: filling out a card that requires some thought, simple math problems, and other normally easy tasks. The purpose of this exercise is to allow them to recognize symptoms of hypoxia, and to know the steps for treatment. In all cases, the procedure is to replace the mask and select 100% oxygen.

The most common symptoms are a slight headache, a feeling of warmth, and tunnel vision. Although it sometimes takes several minutes for pilots to recognize the symptoms, it takes only a single breath of 100% oxygen to completely restore vision to a complete depth of field, with brilliant color and focus.

Spiritual hypoxia can strike any one of us from Monday to Saturday. We can get caught up in all kinds of issues at work, school, or home that distract us from worshipping God in our lives. Maybe we do not recognize the symptoms – long intervals between prayer, reading from God's word, or fellowshipping with our church.

But, each Sunday we have the opportunity to refocus and remember what God has done for us. At communion, we share the bread and the cup representing spiritual oxygen for our souls. A chance to take a breath gives us focus and places our lives in proper perspective. As we share these emblems this morning, let us remember the gift of our Lord, but also commit ourselves to daily oxygen doses from His Word and prayer.

Redeemed

One of the greatest customer loyalty programs ever invented was S&H Green stamps. At the cash register, purchasers received 1 stamp for every 10 cents they spent, so a trip to the grocery store could yield up to 40 or 50 stamps. After licking and pasting into the stamp books, there was a lot of anticipation looking at the catalog and counting the number of books needed for various items.

Eventually, families would pile into their cars with all their books of stamps and head to the  S&H Redemption Center. For the kids, 'redemption' was a pretty big word, but even they knew it had something to do with taking in a bunch of books of green stamps and walking out with a cool toaster or an electric knife.

It was almost like getting stuff for free. People acted like they paid for the stuff because they turned over books of stamps as payment, but the stuff really did not cost anything. They were bought and paid in full, with stamps that were free.

That whole scheme must have been invented by a Christian who knew God's plan for His people. God had planned all along redeem us. We have been purchased – paid in full - so we would not remain slaves to sin, and we could live forever with Him. Paul explained this to the Colossians in this way: *"For he has rescued us from the dominion of darkness and brought us into the kingdom of the Son he loves, in whom we have redemption, the forgiveness of sins"* (Col 1:13-14).

It is only through the payment God made, by giving His Son on the cross, that we can be redeemed – we have been bought and paid for – but to us it was free.

It is this free gift we remember this morning by sharing communion together.

Home Keys

These days we are all very busy … we go to school; we go to work; we go to sports events; we go to work functions; we go to after school activities; we go to church; we go to Sunday School; we have family activities; we go to small groups. Before you know it, we are running from activity to activity with little opportunity to reflect on where we came from or why we are here.

Paul gives us a very simple reminder of what our foundation should be in 2 Timothy 2:8:

"Remember Jesus Christ, raised from the dead, descended from David. This is my gospel."

One of the great foundational classes in high school used to be typing … with real typewriters!

And one of the first lessons in typing was how to

 put your fingers on the 'Home Keys' with the index fingers on the F and J keys. Once you learned that, everything else made sense and fit together; and you might have even been able to type without looking at the keyboard.

But if you ever accidentally placed your fingers somewhere other than the home keys, you would be in big trouble. You would look down in horror to see a bunch of hieroglyphics on the page – just a bunch of jumbled letters that did not make any sense at all.

Well, it is one thing to do that to a piece of paper, but it is much more serious when we do that to our lives. We need to regularly check, making sure we are aligned with the 'Home Keys' of our spiritual life.

Paul's simple antidote is to *"Remember Jesus Christ..."* and that is exactly what we are going to do right now. We are going to remember Him in the way He asked us to – through this communion celebration.

A Veteran's Salute

Everyone today is familiar with the now famous date of 9/11. But before that, the most famous date and time in American history was 11/11/11. At 11:00 AM, on the 11th day of the 11th month in 1918, the war to end all wars was formally ended. To commemorate that event and honor all veterans who have served our country, Nov 11th has been designated Veterans Day.

Veterans Day is significant because of what our veterans have done for us:

- They have left the safety of home in order to save others.

- They have forsaken the comfort of home to suffer in a foreign land.

- Many have paid with their lives for a cause they believed in.

It is good and honorable to honor our veterans and we should be proud to live in such a country. But, their example of service and sacrifice is made perfect in a man who once said:

"I am the good shepherd; the good shepherd gives

his life for the sheep" (John 10:11).

He also said: "*Greater love has no man than this, that he would lay down his life for his friends*" (John 15:13).

Jesus was not drafted or commanded to come to this earth. He left the safety of heaven to save others; He forsook the comfort of living as God to come live with man to a sinful earth, and He went to the cross for a cause He believed in ... the need to reunite us with God by cleansing us of our sins.

Maybe most people in America no longer remember 11/11/11. And it is possible our children or grandchildren will not remember 9/11. But by the grace of God, we will always remember the sacrifice of our Lord on the cross. And we do that right now by sharing in this time of communion.

Ebenezer

Many people hear the name "Ebenezer" and think of Scrooge from the Charles Dickens story "A Christmas Carol." But, Ebenezer is actually a great name from the Bible taken from the book of 1 Samuel.

As was common in those days, the Israelites were fighting the Philistines and suffered a defeat. They thought *"why not bring the ark of the covenant into battle so that it will save us from our enemies?"* Unfortunately, the Israelites were  soundly defeated in that battle, losing 30,000 soldiers along with the ark. The Israelites thought of the ark as some sort of a good luck charm protecting them, not realizing that although it represented God – it was not God. So the ark was carried into captivity where it plagued the Philistines for 7 months, before they sent it back to the Israelites. Eventually, the Philistines marshaled their forces for another attack. But, this time the Israelites repented of their sins and idolatry. We are told they *"served the Lord only.*" When the Israelites prevailed over the Philistines, Samuel set up a stone at that place and named it Ebenezer, meaning stone of help – a reminder of God's love and redemption.

You may remember the words of the great hymn, "Come, Thou Fount of Every Blessing":

> Here I raise mine Ebenezer,
> Hither by Thy help I'm come,
> And I hope, by Thy good pleasure,
> Safely to arrive at home.
> Jesus sought me when a stranger,
> Wand'ring from the fold of God;
> He, to rescue me from danger,
> Interposed His precious blood.

Like the Ark of the Covenant, the emblems of the Lord's Supper are not God, nor do they have the power of God. But, they do point us to God and the sacrifice of His son. It is not this supper, but Jesus himself who is our Ebenezer – our stone of help. He alone can atone for our sin and restore us before the Father. Let us remember Him this morning in the manner He requested.

Hosanna!

On Palm Sunday we look back in time and remember how Jesus entered Jerusalem. Listen to how John records this event in John 12:12:

The next day the great crowd that had come for the Feast heard that Jesus was on his way to Jerusalem. They took palm branches and went out to meet him, shouting, Hosanna! Blessed is he who comes in the name of the Lord. Blessed is the King of Israel!

The shouts of "*Hosanna! Blessed is he who comes in the name of the Lord*" were not as spontaneous as they may have sounded from the text. The Jews were very familiar with the phrase from Psalm 118:25. They were required to recite it once a day during the Feast of the Tabernacles. They recited it as a people aware of God's promises and looking forward to the coming Messiah.

Hosanna was a very strong word, which today would be translated save us – save us now! So the people greeted Jesus as their Messiah and shouted to Him to "save us – save us now!"

Jesus answered their plea four days later in the privacy of an upper room, when He celebrated the Passover supper with His disciples.

While they were eating, Jesus took bread, gave thanks and broke it, and gave it to his disciples, saying, "Take and eat; this is my body." Then he took the cup, gave thanks and offered it to them, saying, "Drink from it, all of you. This is my blood of the covenant, which is poured out for many for the forgiveness of sins" (Matthew 26:26-28).

The Jews cried "Save us!" and Jesus responded saying here is my blood, which is for the forgiveness of sins.

This morning we will share in the Lord's Supper commemorating His sacrifice on the cross. And we do not need to shout Hosanna – Save us, save us now! Instead, we can, in all confidence, proclaim … Jesus has saved us indeed!

Puzzle Pieces

If you are one of those who like to put together jigsaw puzzles, you know they come in boxes of 500 to 1500 pieces looking remarkably alike. A novice puzzle maker might quickly become discouraged by the overwhelming number of pieces and no clear instructions on how to get started.

 Well, apparently there is a successful strategy to putting together difficult puzzles. It goes something like this: first you turn all the pieces face up. Then, you select the edge pieces and finally group colored sections by referring to the finished picture on the box.

Imagine how hard it would be to put together a puzzle, if we left all the pieces face down? Sometimes, that is exactly how we try to live our lives, and we find ourselves strewn about everywhere, not sure how to start putting ourselves back to together. 1 Corinthians 13:12 reminds us there are some things we do not know about this life: *"Now we see but a poor reflection as in a*

mirror; then we shall see face to face." But, just as in putting together a puzzle … if we get really stuck, we need to look at the picture on the box. The picture for us is the perfect example of Jesus.

Instead of looking at the blank unrecognizable shapes of the problems in our lives, we need to turn them over, not just so we can recognize them, but we need to turn them over to Jesus, so He can intercede on our behalf before God. It is only by doing so, we honor the sacrifice He made for us on the cross; it is only by doing so, we become free to serve God; and, it is only by doing so, our lives have meaning and purpose.

Let us use this time of communion to remember the sacrifice Jesus made on our behalf and turn the pieces of our lives over to Him.

Substitutes – Good or Bad?

I still remember when I decided to go on a diet in the late 70s. The only diet soft drink available was Tab – some sort of cola drink with an artificial sweetener called Saccharin. I think they have changed the recipe since those early days, because that was a sure way to stop a diet before it ever got going. You might as well have ground up a  rusty nail and dissolved it in seltzer water! By any standard, Tab was a poor substitute for those used to drinking Coca Cola.

A host of other substitutes are available today ... margarine instead of butter, soy milk for real milk, yogurt for ice cream, blended mixes for real eggs, plastic for metal, substitute teachers for real teachers, etc. Honestly, I cannot think of any products actually better than the real thing.

But, true to His nature, God takes what seems right to man and makes the opposite true. Abraham learned this lesson when God asked him to offer Isaac up as a burnt offering:

But the angel of the LORD called out to him from heaven, "Abraham! Abraham!" "Here I am," he replied. "Do not lay a hand on the boy," he said. "Do not do anything to him. Now I know that you fear God, because you have not withheld from me your son, your only son." Abraham looked up and there in the thicket he saw a ram caught by its horns. He went over and took the ram and sacrificed it as a burnt offering instead of his son. So Abraham called that place The LORD Will Provide. And to this day it is said, "On the mountain of the LORD it will be provided (Genesis 22:11-14).

God's plan was always to bless man by providing a substitute. For Abraham, God demonstrated this by substituting a ram for his son; for us, God demonstrated this by substituting His son for our sins. Now, we remember and celebrate as we share communion together.

Someone Please Tell Me What To Do!

Maybe you have heard the names Eppie and Pauline Phillips. They grew up in Sioux City, IA, and each one of them ended up writing newspaper columns giving readers advice on what to do in various situations. Eppie was better known as Ann Landers, and her twin sister Pauline wrote "Dear Abby", using the name Abigail Van Buren. Their columns were immensely popular as millions of people asked them for advice on problems concerning life's difficult situations.

God never intended that we be left without guidance or answers on what to do in life. In Old

 Testament times, the high priest used small objects called Urim and Thummim to determine God's will. Although we do not know much about them, some believe they were flat objects, each with a 'yes' and a 'no' side to them. The priest could handle them or

toss them out of the pouch, and God would reveal His message for the people of Israel.

We have come a long way, since the days of David and Samuel and Urim and Thummim. Today, we have God's word and the example of Jesus to guide us through difficult situations. But, the interesting part is the origin of the words: Urim is related to a Hebrew word *ārar* meaning 'to curse' and is used to give a negative answer. Thummim is related to *tāmam*, meaning to be perfect, and is used to answer in the affirmative.

Galatians 3:13 says: *"Christ redeemed us from the curse of the law by becoming a curse for us, for it is written: 'Cursed is everyone who is hung on a tree.'"* It is fascinating that even from the beginning of God's relationship with man He used the idea of something cursed and something perfect to reveal His will. His plan has always been to use the perfect to cure the cursed, the sinless to cover the sins of the guilty, which is the answer God wants us to seek and remember, especially during this time of communion.

The Maltese Cross

A group of crusaders called the Knights of St. John encountered a new weapon while fighting for the holy land. The defenders hurled glass containers of naphtha into the advancing crusaders followed by a flaming torch. As the survivors risked their lives to save their burning comrades, they became our first fire fighters and received a badge of honor recognizing their sacrifice on the battlefield for their comrades.

Because the knights lived on the island of Malta, their badge became known as the Maltese Cross, and the background shape for the badge worn by today's firefighters. The Maltese Cross is still a symbol of sacrifice and protection, as firefighters continue to lay down their lives to save victims from fire and disaster.

God tells us that we are made in His image. We have the same spiritual DNA, and it is not unusual to hear of someone sacrificing for another. It is a trait I believe we inherited from our heavenly

Father ... a trait made perfect in His son. Jesus says in John 15: 13: *"Greater love has no one than this, that he lay down his life for his friends. You are my friends if you do what I command."*

Just like the Maltese Cross has become a symbol of the bravery and sacrifice of our fire fighters, this communion service is a symbol of the greatest gift of sacrifice.

As we take the bread, we remember the body of our Lord, beaten and pierced as He suffered on the cross. And as we take the cup, we remember the blood that Jesus shed to cover our sins.

General Orders No. 11

It started during the Civil War, when the ladies in the south began decorating the graves of their fallen soldiers. As this practice spread, it was officially recognized by the commander of the Grand Army of the Republic, General John Logan. Here are excerpts of his General Order Number 11:

> The 30th day of May, 1868, is designated for the purpose of strewing with flowers or otherwise decorating the graves of comrades who died in defense of their country ... In this observance no form of ceremony is prescribed, but posts and comrades will in their own way arrange such fitting services and testimonials of respect as circumstances may permit. ... It is the purpose of the Commander-in-Chief to inaugurate this observance with the hope that it will be kept up from year to year, while a survivor of the war remains to honor the memory of his departed comrades.

I am very happy we have a holiday to remember our military members who have given their lives for our country. It makes it even more fitting that we have a memorial for Jesus, the Son of God, who gave His live for all of mankind. Although Gen Logan specified there was to be no form of ceremony prescribed, Jesus gave us very specific instructions about how to remember Him in Matthew 26:

> *While they were eating, Jesus took bread, gave thanks and broke it and gave it to his disciple saying, "Take and eat; this is my body." Then he took the cup, gave thanks and offered it to them saying, "Drink from it, all of you. This is my blood of the covenant, which is poured out for many for the forgiveness of sins.*

Every memorial needs some longevity. General Logan asked that as long as a survivor of the war remained alive, he should honor the memory of his fallen comrades. And as Christians, we hold a similar very sacred trust: The Lord's Supper was instituted by Jesus himself. It is our honor to observe it whenever we meet to worship, and it is our responsibility to teach our children its observance and meaning.

Those Are My Men Down There!

P robably not many of you will recognize the name of Bruce Crandall. Major Bruce Crandall was an Army helicopter pilot in Vietnam. On November 14, 1965, Major Crandall was transporting a battalion of soldiers when they came under intense attack during one of his landings. Major Crandall kept his helicopter on the ground until 4 of the wounded soldiers could be loaded aboard and flown back to his base.

For the next 14 hours, he flew back into what they called the Valley of Death ... ferrying badly needed supplies inbound and carrying the wounded out.  Flying 3 different helicopters, since the first 2 were so badly damaged, he ended up evacuating some 70 wounded soldiers and saved the battalion from being completely overrun.

Acknowledged as a hero and awarded the Medal of Honor, Major Crandall simply observed: "There was never any consideration that we would not go into those landing zones. They were my people down there, and they trusted me to come and get them."

In John 6:38 – 41, Jesus explains to His disciples and to us, why He left heaven to come to earth:

For I have come down from heaven not to do my will but to do the will of him who sent me. And this is the will of him who sent me, that I shall lose none of all that he has given me, but raise them up at the last day. For my Father's will is that everyone who looks to the Son and believes in him shall have eternal life, and I will raise him up at the last day.

When I read that, I know there was never any consideration that Jesus would not come to earth for us. And I can imagine Him telling the Father, "Those are my people down there, and they trust me to come and save them."

So He did. Now we have the privilege of remembering His sacrifice for us as we share together this bread representing His body, and this juice representing His blood, shed to cover our sins.

The Disease of Not Remembering

In 1907, a German doctor published observations of one of his patients who had experienced serious problems with her memory. He described a terrible disease of 'not remembering' ... a disease causing people to forget what is important, to forget who they are, and to forget what has happened before. The man's name was Dr. Alois Alzheimer.

The tragedy of this disease is that our God is a God of remembering. God *remembered* Noah; God *remembered* Rachel; God heard His people groaning in slavery and *remembered* His covenant with Abraham, Isaac, and Jacob. Time and time again, we see God remembering in the scriptures. As our creator, God created us in His image, and in this case, with an innate, hard-wired desire to remember things. No one has to tell us to remember our children's birthdays; no one has to tell us to remember our anniversaries; no one has to tell us to remember other special days like Sep 11th, Veterans' Day, or Valentine's Day. Like God, we remember. So as His people, we remember what is important –we are here to glorify Him; we remember who we are – God's children; we remember what has happened before – He gave His only Son as a sacrifice for our sins, and gave us a memorial to observe as we remember.

> *For I received from the Lord what I also passed on to you: The Lord Jesus, on the night he was betrayed, took bread, and when he had given thanks, he broke it and said, "This is my body, which is for you; do this in remembrance of me." In the same way, after supper he took the cup, saying, "This cup is the new covenant in my blood; do this, whenever you drink it, in remembrance of me." For whenever you eat this bread and drink this cup, you proclaim the Lord's death until he comes* (1 Corinthians 11:23-26).

The Arranged Marriage

As a parent I have sometimes joked that my children would all have arranged marriages. Then, I would get to select the groom and make sure he measured up to my standards. As funny as that sounds in our culture, arranged marriages are the tradition in other parts of the world such as India. Now you may think this is a recipe for disaster, but, actually, in India only 1% of married couples get divorced compared to 50% in the United States.

We also see arranged marriages in the scriptures, like Isaac's marriage to Rebekah. If you

remember the story from Genesis 24, Abraham sent his servant Eliezer to find a wife for Isaac. As he stood by the well, he prayed God would show His choice by having her agree to get Eliezer and his camels a drink from the well.

God places a high premium on marriages, so it is no surprise that we see His hand in selecting marriage partners. Just as Abraham, the father, sent his servant to find a bride for his son, God sent His servant, the Holy Spirit to find a bride for His Son. As Isaac waited in the Promised Land for His bride to arrive, Jesus now sits at the right hand of the Father, waiting for our reunion with Him.

Hallelujah! For our Lord God Almighty reigns. Let us rejoice and be glad and give him glory! For the wedding of the Lamb has come, and his bride has made herself ready. Fine linen, bright and clean, was given her to wear (Revelations 19: 6-8).

Until the wedding, the bridegroom has left us the gift of these communion emblems ... the bread that represents His body offered as a sacrifice, and the cup representing His blood given for the forgiveness of sins. Let us then make ourselves ready for the marriage by living holy lives worthy of the sacrifice given for us.

The Clean Sweep

When I was growing up, I remember going with my parents to buy the only new car they ever purchased. One of the critical components in the decision was choosing a color that would not show dirt -- in other words, no white or black cars. The car still got dirty … it just meant I did not have to wash it as often. In much the same way over the years, I have heard my wife proclaim the virtues of carpet whose color and texture combine marvelously to hide dirt.

Why is it we are so obsessed with hiding the dirt, and not as concerned with keeping every spec of dirt off our car or carpet? I believe it is because we know they will end up getting dirty. Cars drive on dirty roads – they are going to get dirty. People and pets walk on the carpet – it is going to get dirty. So we concern ourselves with how to hide the dirt so we do not have to clean quite so often.

I think God knew that in our personal lives, we would get ourselves mired in the dirt of sin. But, unlike us, God did not spend any time whatsoever trying to figure out how to create us so the sin did not show. Instead of trying to hide our sins and keep them from showing, God shined a brilliant light on them through the truth of His Word. Then, He set about removing every particle, every spec of dirt by sending His Son to pay for our sins. Because Jesus went to the cross, our sins are not hidden – they are forgiven. We are no longer dirty, but clean and white as snow. *"Though your sins are like scarlet, they shall be as white as snow; though they are red as crimson, they shall be like wool"* (Isaiah 1:18-19).

This is the message we have heard from him and declare to you: God is light; in him there is no darkness at all. If we claim to have fellowship with him yet walk in the darkness, we lie and do not live by the truth. But if we walk in the light, as he is in the light, we have fellowship with one another, and the blood of Jesus, his Son, purifies us from all sin (John 1:7-9).

Healed by a Snake

Ophidiophobia describes people who have a fear of snakes. It is not that they just do not like snakes or are afraid of being bitten by them. People with Ophidiophobia do not even like to think about snakes, see them on TV, or in pictures. If you remember Indiana Jones, he had a pretty bad case of Ophidiophobia.

The nation of Israel had every right to be afraid of snakes. As they were traveling to the Red Sea, they began to complain about their travels, *"we don't have water, we don't have bread, and we hate this food."* God heard their grumbling and sent poisonous snakes among them and many of them were bitten and died. The people quickly repented and asked Moses to pray for relief. God instructed Moses to make a bronze snake and put it on a pole, so anyone who had been bitten, but looked at the bronze snake, would live.

Notice that God did not take away the snakes, but He did provide the cure for their venom. The interesting part about this imagery is that many medical symbols today contain the Rod of  Asclepius – a rod with a serpent wrapped around it, and a well-known symbol of medical healing and assistance to the sick. But God had much more important imagery in mind when He told Moses to construct the serpent. Here is how Jesus explained it to Nicodemus:

I have spoken to you of earthly things and you do not believe; how then will you believe if I speak of heavenly things? No one has ever gone into heaven except the one who came from heaven—the Son of Man. Just as Moses lifted up the snake in the desert, so the Son of Man must be lifted up, that everyone who believes in him may have eternal life (John 3:10-15).

Just as the nation of Israel obeyed God and was healed, let us look on Jesus this morning, and see Him lifted up on the cross for our sins. Then, we are healed as well.

CPSIA information can be obtained at www.ICGtesting.com
Printed in the USA
BVOW08s1200251015

423466BV00001BA/107/P